Joplin

SELECTED RAGS TRANSCRIBED for GUITAR

ARRANGED BY NATHANIEL GUNOD

AN ALFRED CLASSICAL GUITAR MASTERWORK EDITION

Cover art: Sheet music covers
The Entertainer *(1902),* Sunflower Slow Drag
(1901), and Peacherine Rag *(1901)*
printed by John Stark & Son
Maple Leaf Rag *(1911), and* Kismet Rag *(1913)*
printed by Stark Music Co.
Weeping Willow Ragtime Two Step *(1903)*
printed by Val. A. Reis Music Co.

Library of Congress, Music Division

Alfred Music
P.O. Box 10003
Van Nuys, CA 91410-0003
alfred.com

Copyright © MMXV by Alfred Music
All rights reserved. Printed in USA.

ISBN-10: 1-4706-1788-9
ISBN-13: 978-1-4706-1788-2

SCOTT JOPLIN

Contents

Preface

Scott Joplin was born in Texas around 1867 or 1868; no one knows for sure exactly when. When he was young, his family left the farm on which his father (formerly a slave) worked as a laborer and moved to Texarkana, which straddles the Texas-Arkansas border. There are stories that the young Scott had access to a piano in a white-owned home where his mother worked, and taught himself the rudiments of music. His talent was noticed by a local music teacher (Julius Weiss), who instructed him, placing special emphasis on European art forms, including opera. This teacher's influence may have been behind Joplin's deep desire for recognition as a classical composer.

There is evidence that between 1891 and 1895 he was beginning his musical career, playing with a minstrel group, leading a band, playing a cornet and traveling with a vocal group called the Texas Medley Quartette. His travels brought him to Syracuse, New York where he impressed two businessmen that published his songs "Please Say You Will" and "A Picture of Her Face."

He worked in Sedalia as a pianist, playing at various events and sites, including the town's two social clubs for black men, the Maple Leaf and Black 400 clubs. He also taught several of the local young musicians in town, most notably Scott Hayden and Arthur Marshall, with whom he later collaborated composing rags.

In 1896 he published two marches and a waltz. Late in 1898 he tried to publish his first two piano rags, but succeeded in selling only "Original Rags." This publication experience was not ideal as he was forced to share credit with a staff arranger. Before Joplin published his next rag, he obtained the assistance and guidance of a lawyer. In August 1899 they contracted with Sedalia music store owner and publisher John Stark to publish "The Maple Leaf Rag," which was to become the greatest and most famous of piano rags. The contract gave Joplin a one-cent royalty on each sale, which gave him a small, but steady income for the rest of his life.

Among Joplin's significant publications were "Sunflower Slow Drag" (a collaboration with Scott Hayden), "Peacherine Rag," "The Easy Winners," "Cleopha," "The Strenuous Life" (a tribute to President Theodore Roosevelt), "A Breeze from Alabama," "Elite Syncopations," "The Entertainer," and "The Ragtime Dance."

Early in 1903 he filed a copyright application for an opera, *A Guest of Honor*. He formed an opera company, rehearsed the work in St. Louis, and embarked on a tour. Early in the tour, someone stole the box office receipts. The tour ended with Joplin unable to meet his payroll. Furthermore, all of his possessions, including the music from the opera, were confiscated. Copies of the score were never filed with the Library of Congress and the music has never been recovered.

Through the next few years his career seems to have floundered and, having lost much of his money on the failed opera, he was in a poor financial condition. In the summer of 1907 Joplin went to New York to make contacts with new publishers and to find financial backing for *Treemonisha*, an opera he had been working on for the past few years.

Joplin set about to arrange a performance of the opera, but he was unsuccessful. Through the next four years, he announced several full productions, but none were realized. In 1911, he mounted an unstaged run-through with piano accompaniment, but it failed to win him the financial backing he sought. Joplin was never to witness a completely staged performance of his opera. By 1916, Joplin was very ill and by mid-January, 1917, he had to be hospitalized and was soon transferred to a mental institution where he died on April 1, 1917.

Signs, Symbols, and Terms

Roman Numerals		
I **1**	V **5**	IX **9**
II **2**	VI **6**	X **10**
III **3**	VII **7**	XI **11**
IV **4**	VIII **8**	XII **12**

> `>` = **Accent**. Emphasize the note.

`{` = **Arpeggiate**. Quickly "roll" the chord.

`Λ` = **Marcato**. Emphasize more than an accent.

BV3 = Barre three strings at the 5th fret.

BV = Barre all six strings at the 5th fret.

HBV = Hinge barre at the 5th fret. Play an individual note on the 1st string with the bottom of the 1st finger, just above the palm. Usually simplifies the next fingering.

⑥ = D = Tune the 6th string down to D

p, i, m, a = The right-hand fingers starting with the thumb.

1, 2, 3, 4, 0 = The left-hand fingers starting with the index finger, and the open string.

adagio = A slow tempo which is faster than *largo* and slower than *andante*.

allegro = Cheerful, quick or fast.

allegretto = A lively quick tempo that moves more slowly than *allegro*.

andante = A moderate, graceful tempo, slower than *allegretto* and faster than *adagio*.

a tempo = Return to the original tempo.

cantabile = Singing.

commodo = Comfortable, leisurely.

con brio = With vigor.

con moto = With motion.

cresc. = Abbreviation for *crescendo*. Gradually becoming louder.

D.C. al Fine = *Da capo al fine*. Go back to the beginning of the piece and play to the *Fine*, which is the end of the piece.

dim. = Abbreviation for *diminuendo*. Gradually becoming softer.

dolce = Sweet.

gliss. = Abbreviation for *glissando*. To slide from one note to another. Often shown as a diagonal line with an S (slide) in guitar music.

harm. = Abbreviation for *harmonic*. Notes of the harmonic series that are very pure and clear. In this book, written at the sounding pitch with a diamond shaped note head. Touch the string lightly directly over the indicated fret and pluck, immediately removing the finger from the string.

largo = Very slow and broad.

legato = Smooth, connected.

leggiero = Light or delicate.

l.v. = Abbreviation for *laissez vibre* (let vibrate).

maestoso = Sublime or magnificent.

moderato = In a moderate tempo.

molto = Very or much.

non troppo = But not too much so.

più = More.

poco a poco = Little by little.

rall. = Abbreviation for *rallentando*. Becoming gradually slower.

rit. = Abbreviation for *ritardando*. Becoming gradually slower.

sempre = Always.

sostenuto = Sustained.

staccato = Short, detached.

tranquillo = Tranquil, calm, quiet.

vivace = Lively, quick.

The Entertainer
A Rag Time Two Step

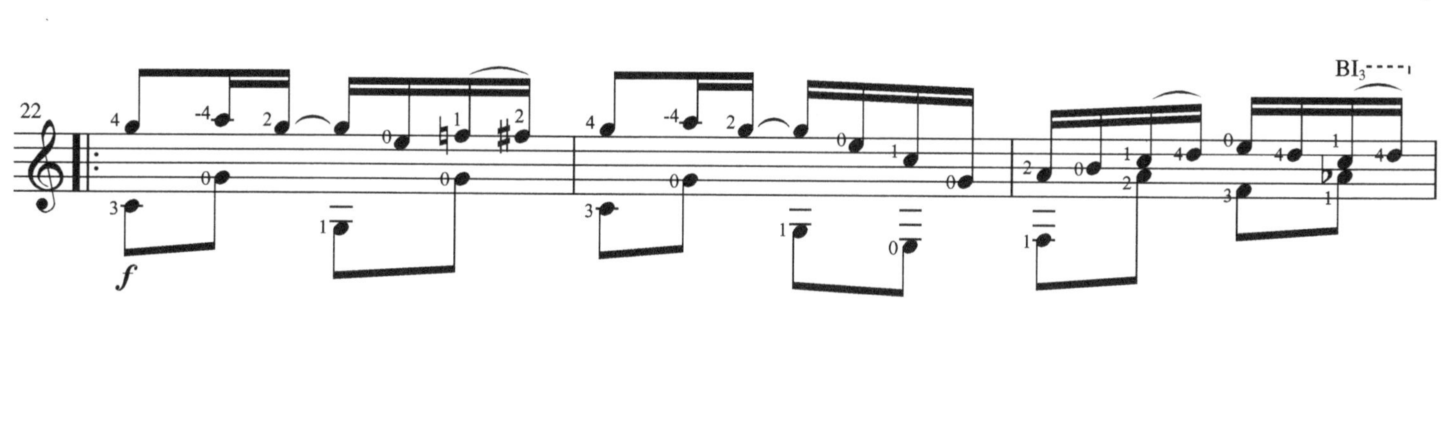

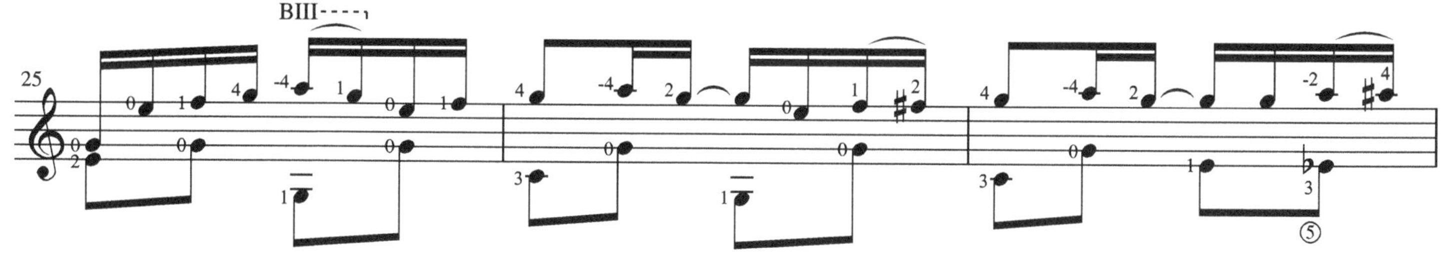

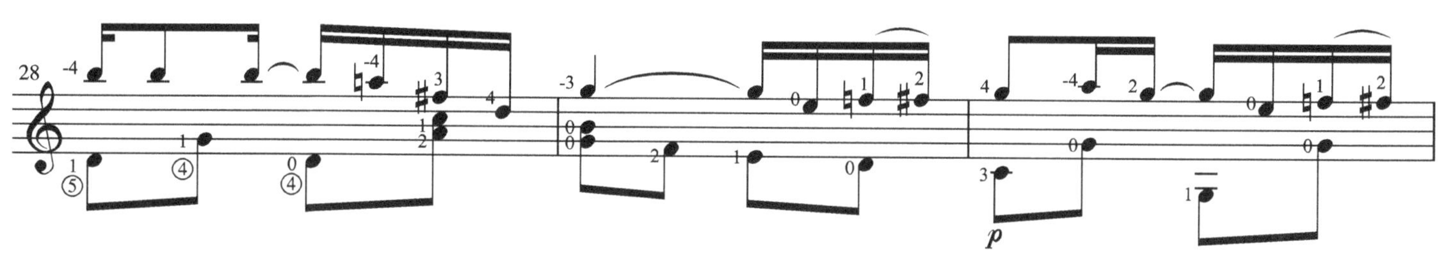

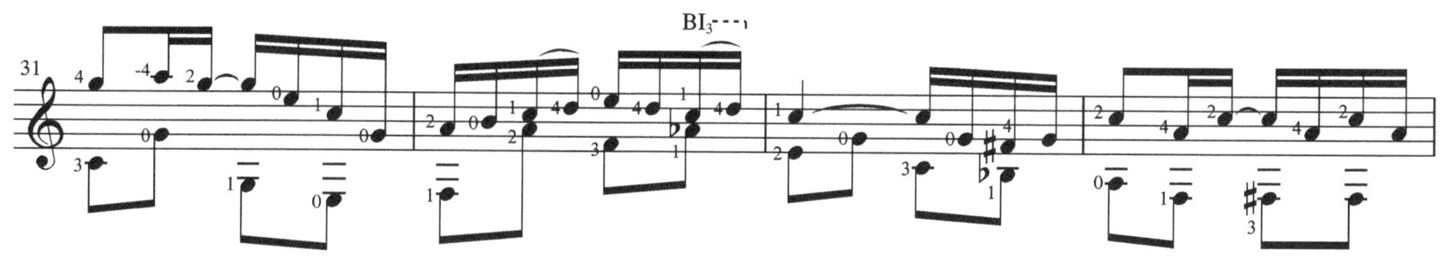

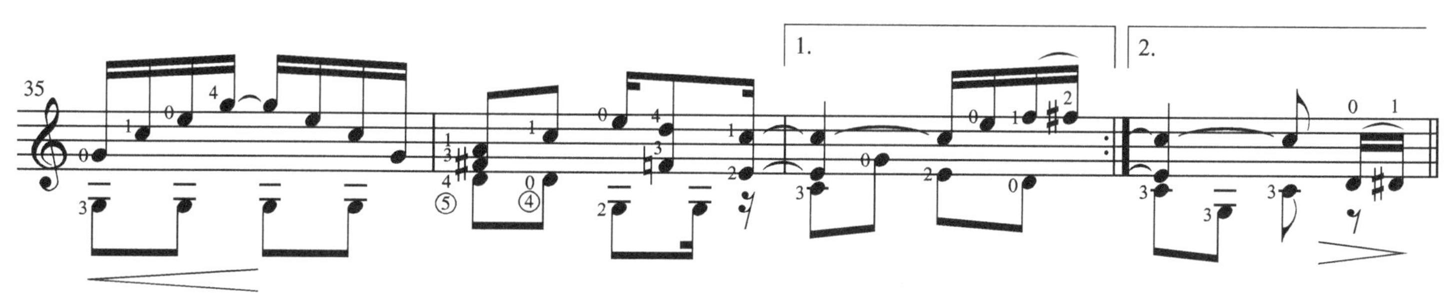

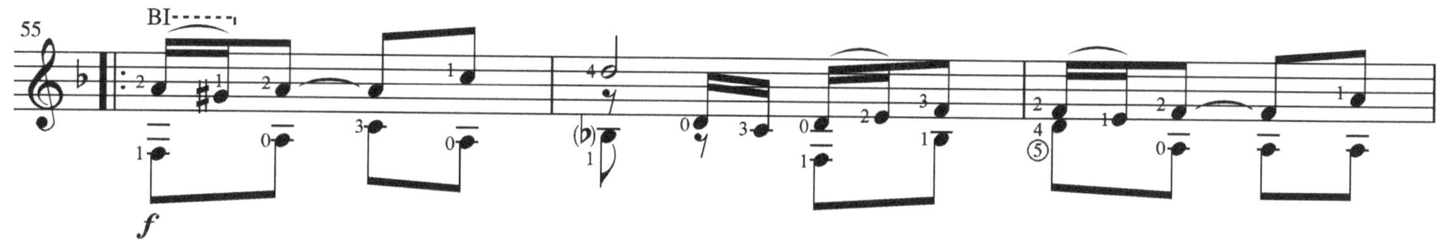

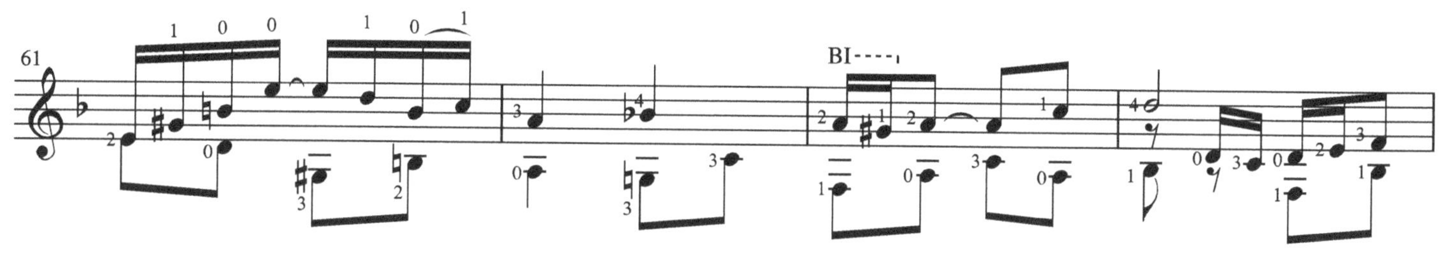

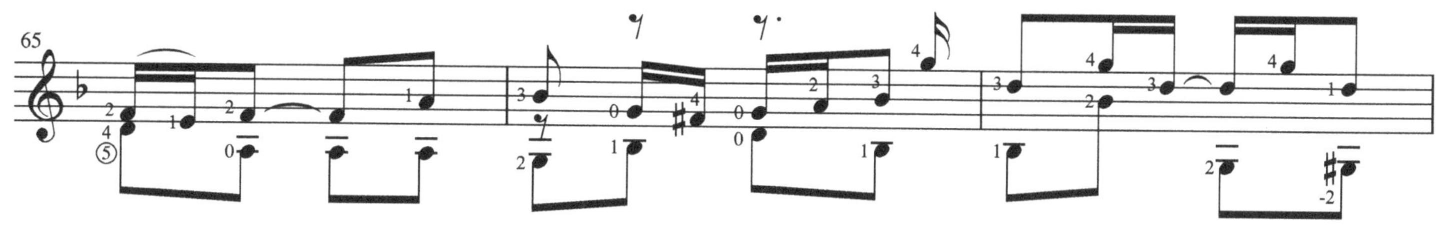

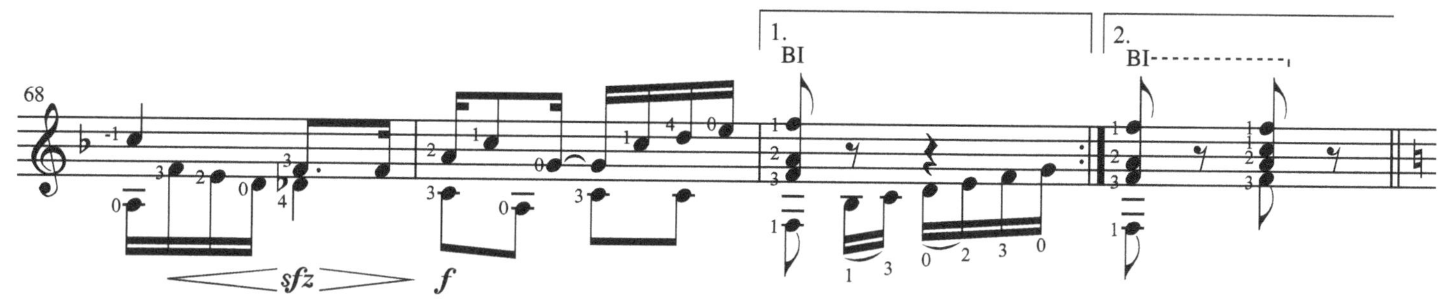

Maple Leaf Rag

35
f
38
41
Harm.
V
8va
p
mf
44
BVIII5 - 1
47

Trio
51
54
57
59
BII₅
62
65
1.
2.
BV₅

68
HBV
BIII₅
72
75
HBV
BIII₅
78
BIII₂
82
1.
BIII₂
2.

Sunflower Slow Drag

A Rag Time Two Step

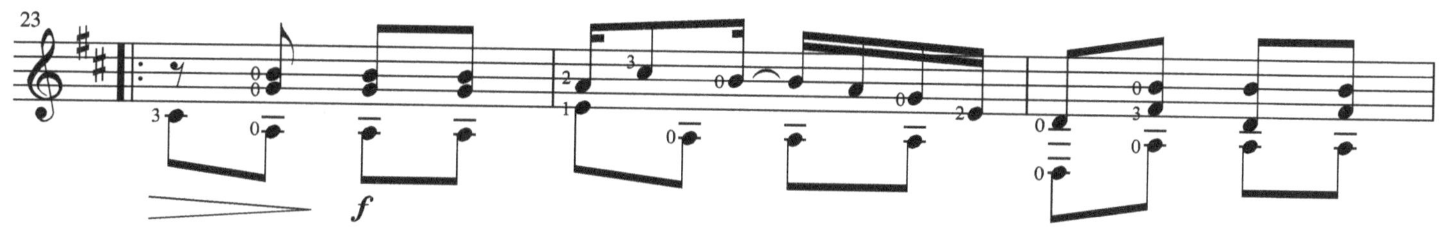

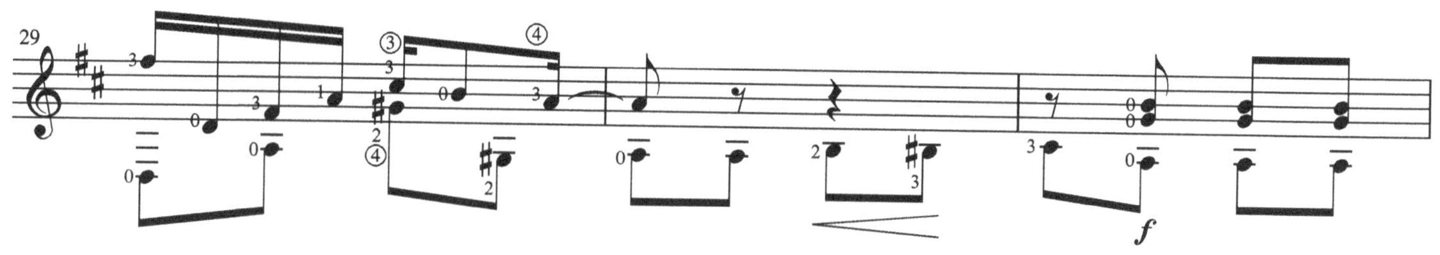

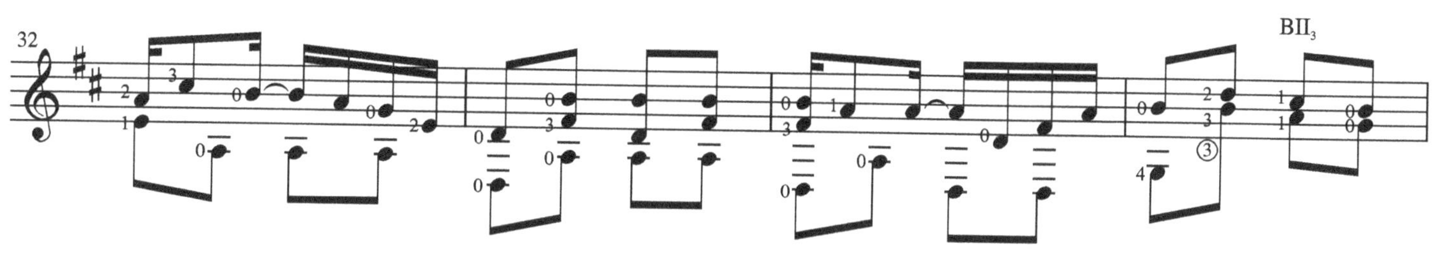

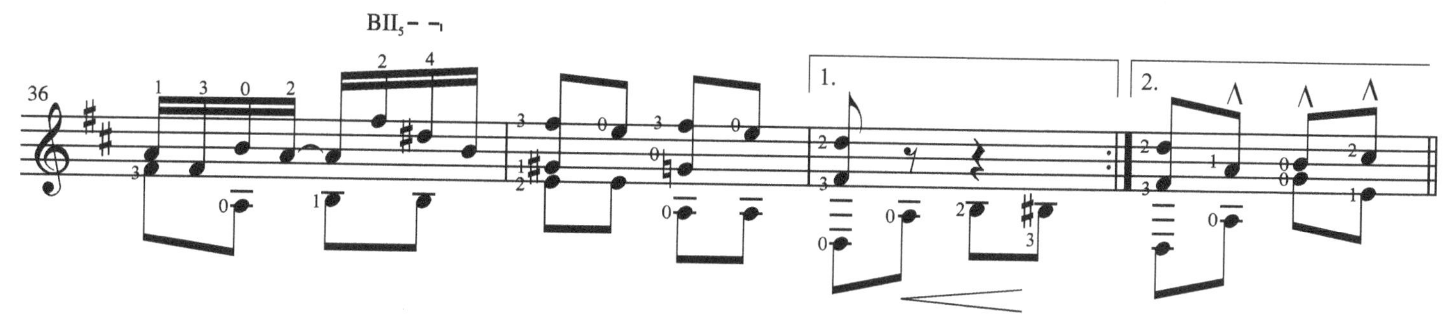

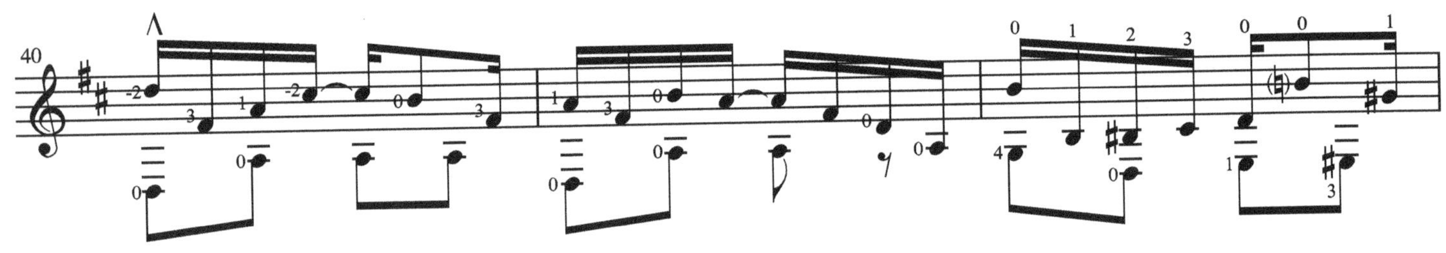

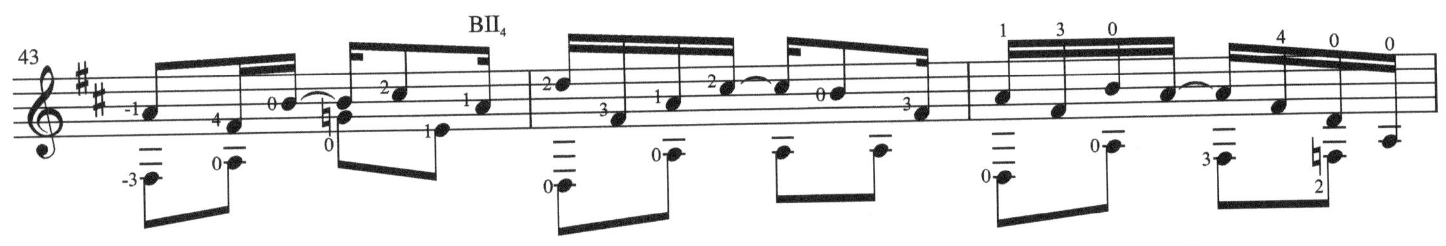

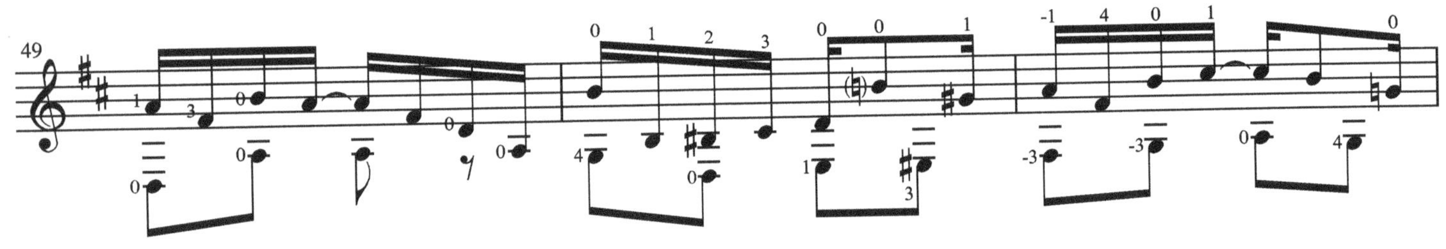

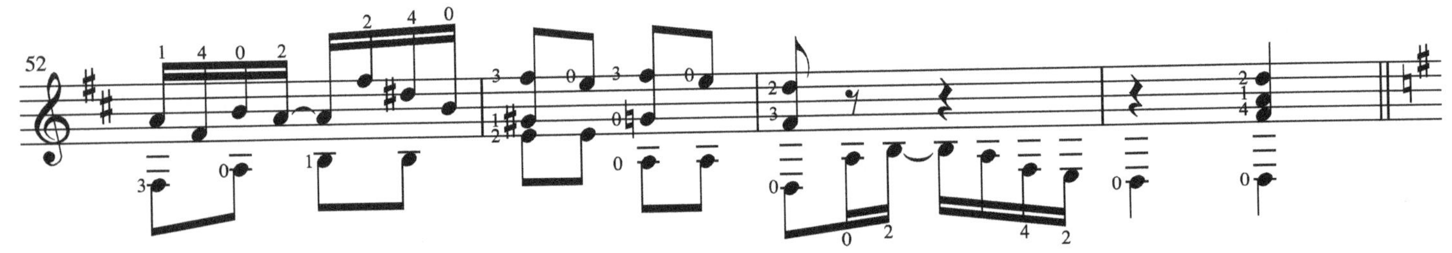

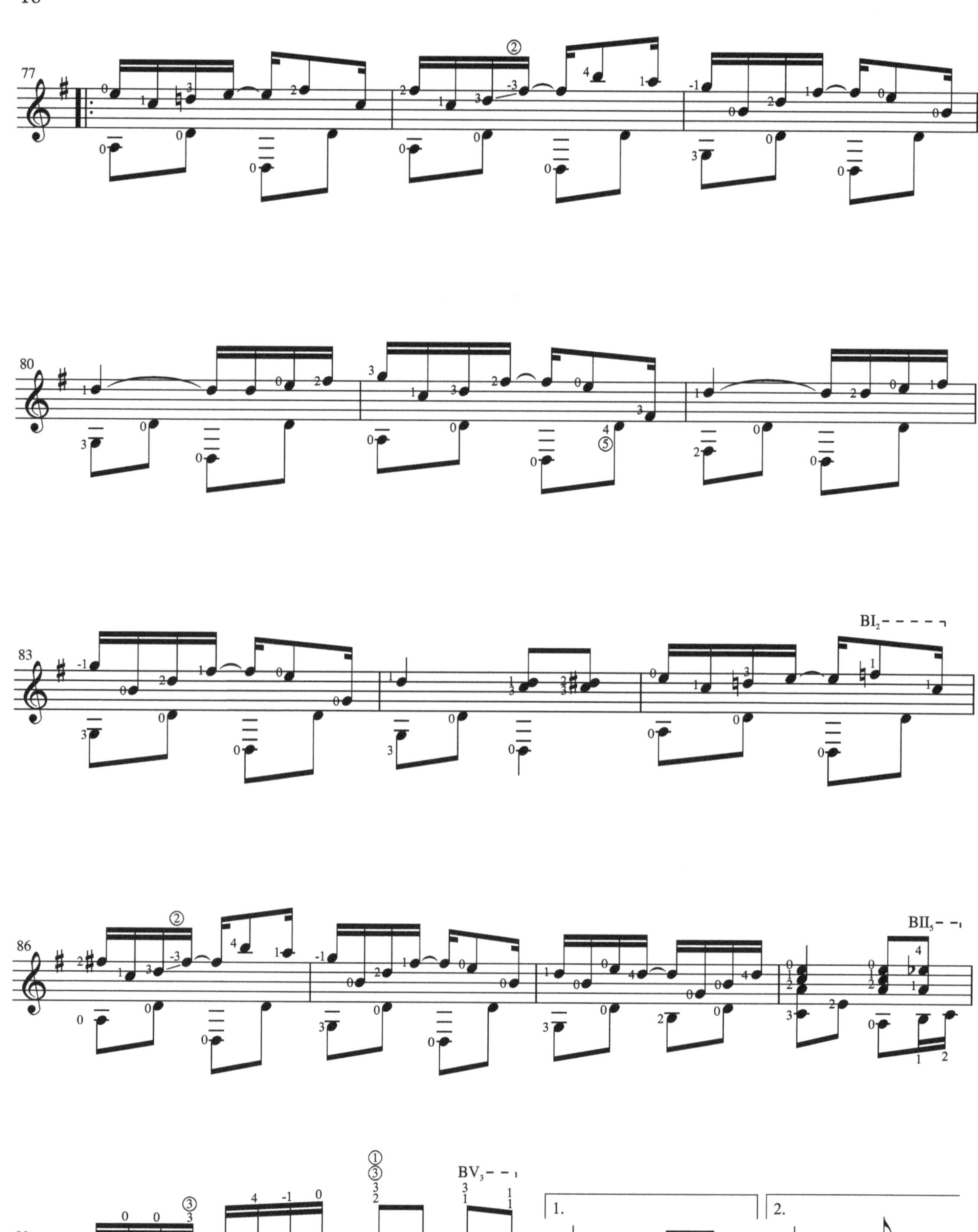

77
80
83
86
90
BI₂
BII₅
BV₃
1.
2.

Weeping Willow
A Rag Time Two Step

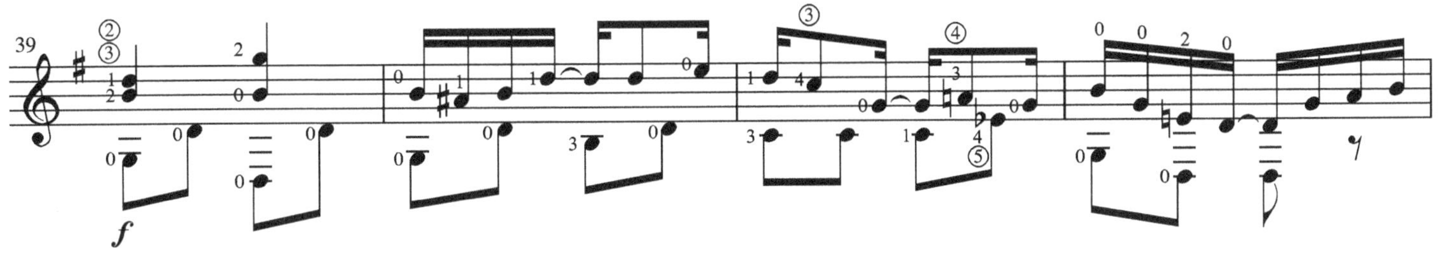

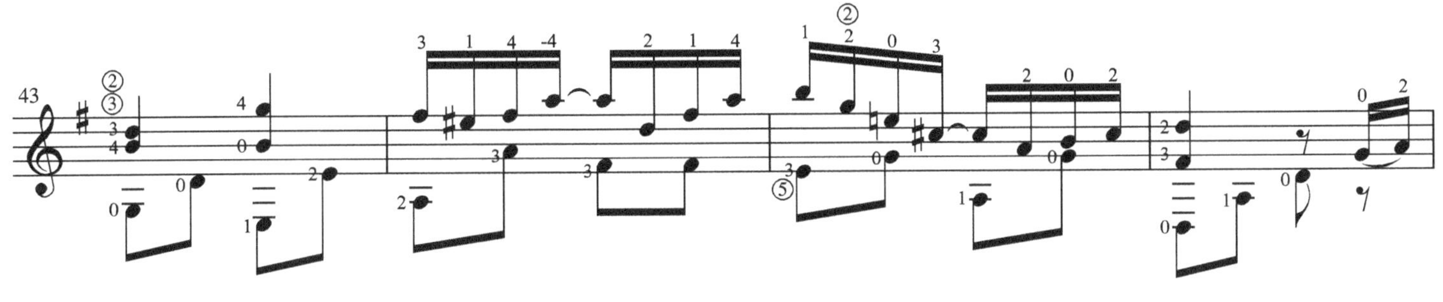

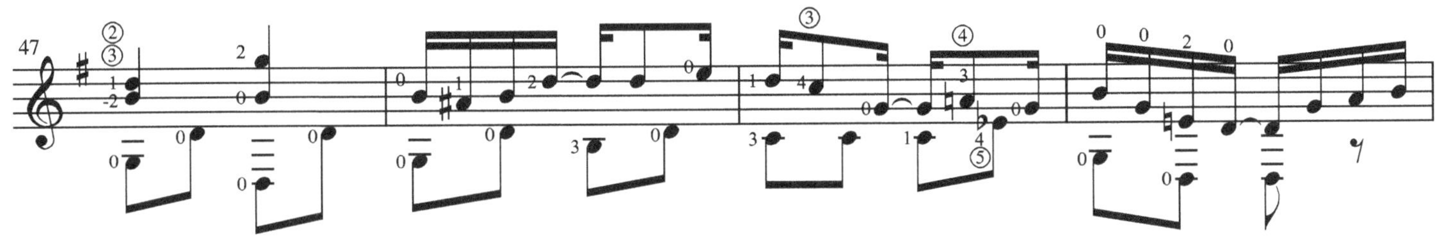

BIV
BII
HBIII
HBII

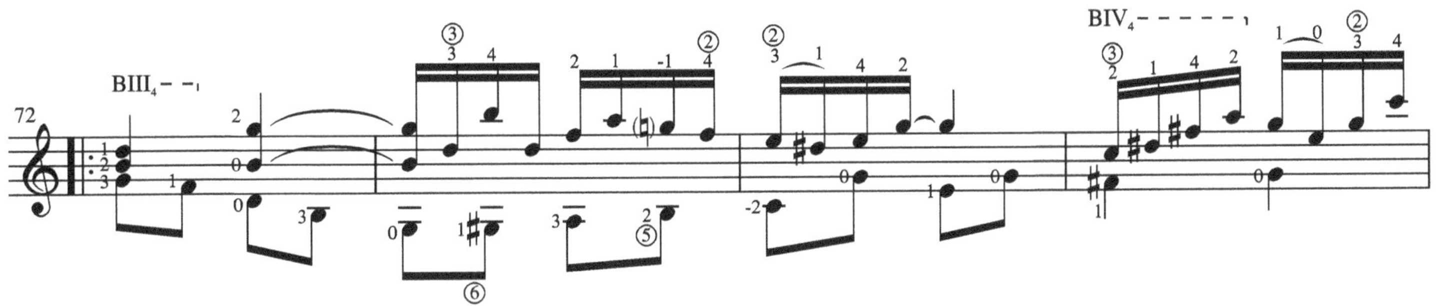

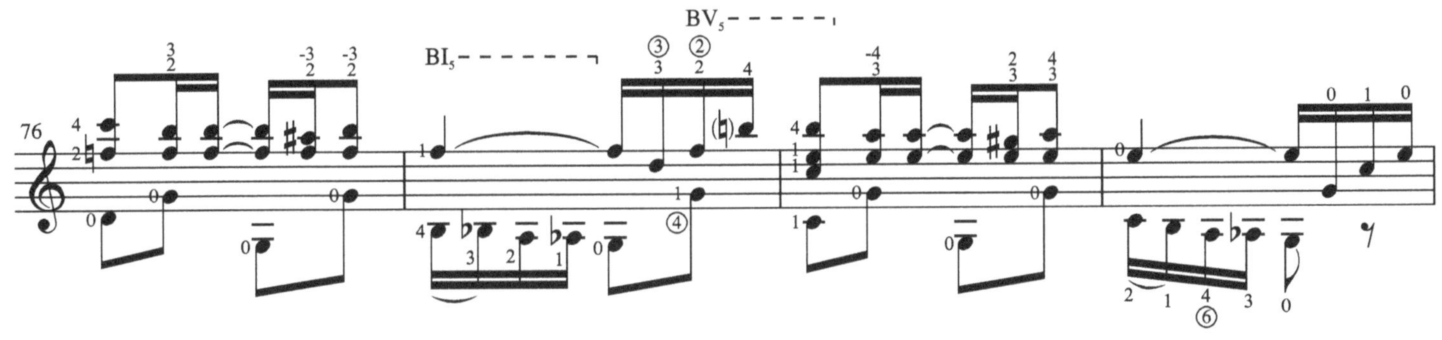

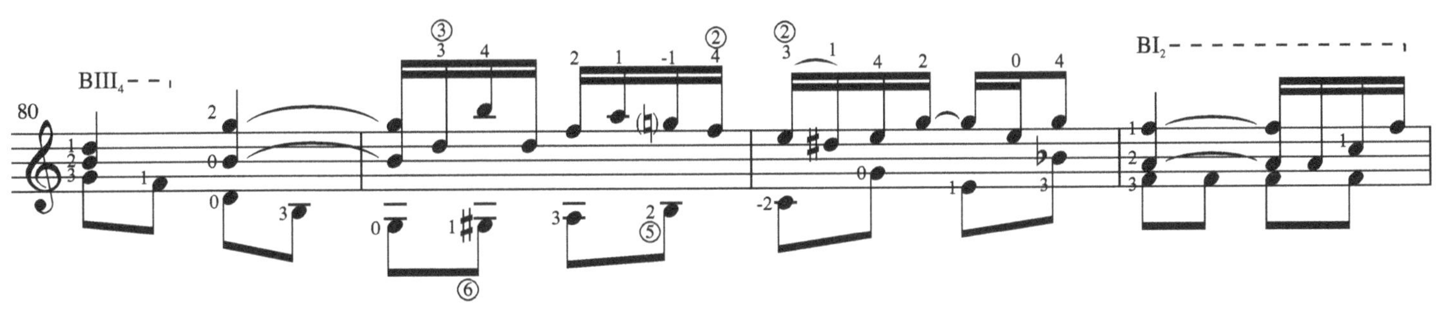

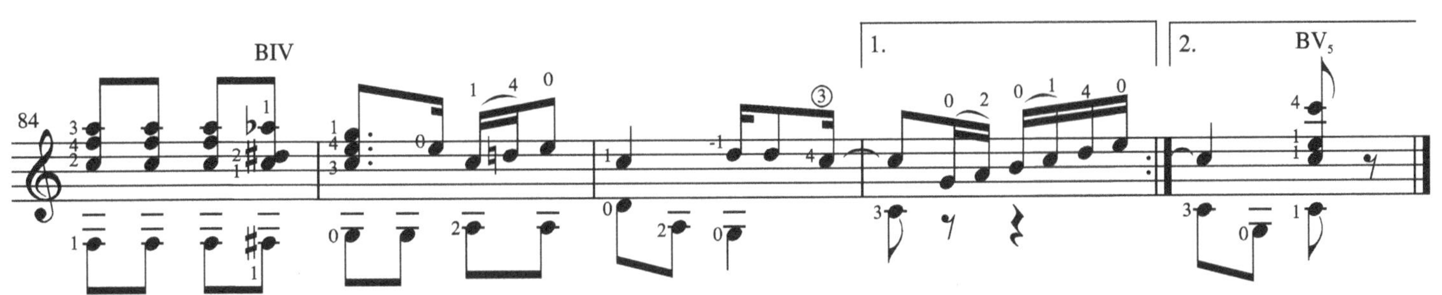

Peacherine Rag

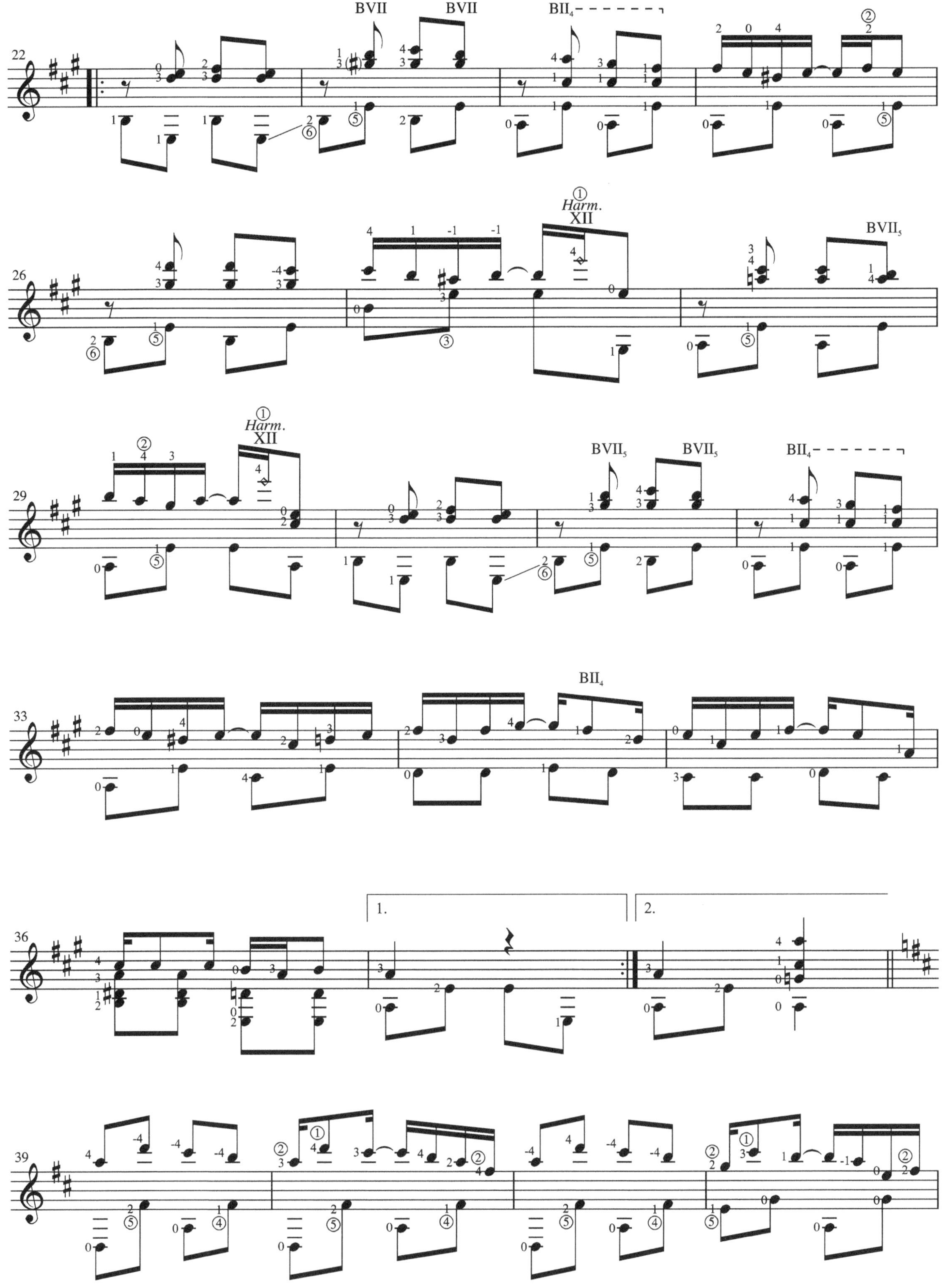

Kismet Rag

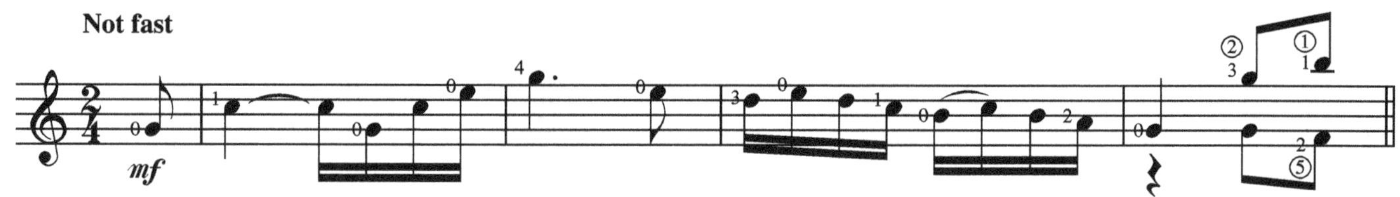

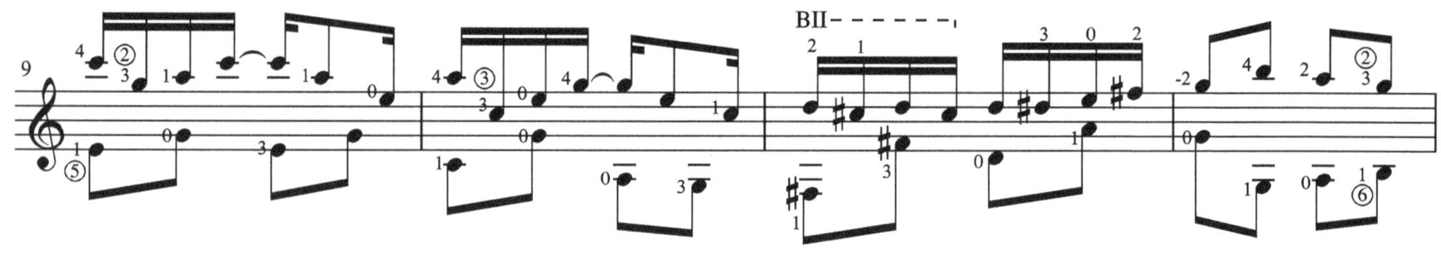

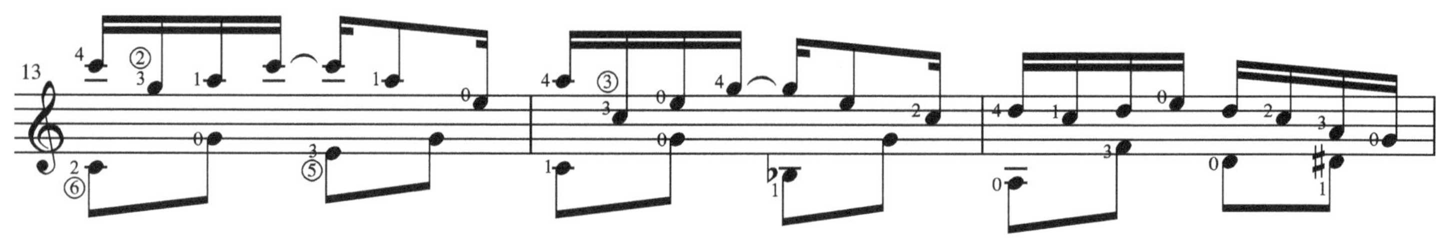

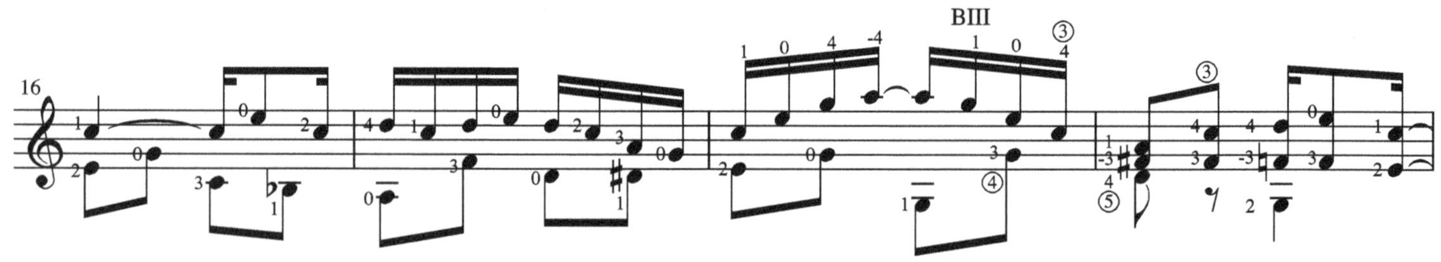

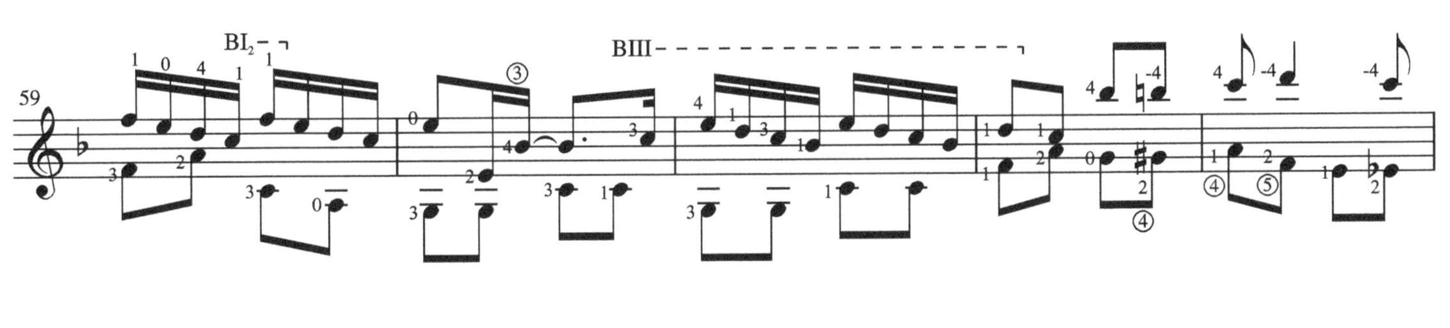

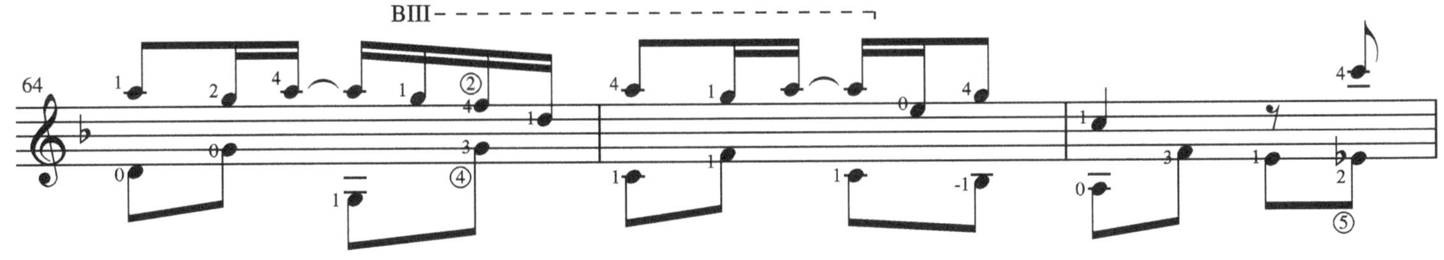

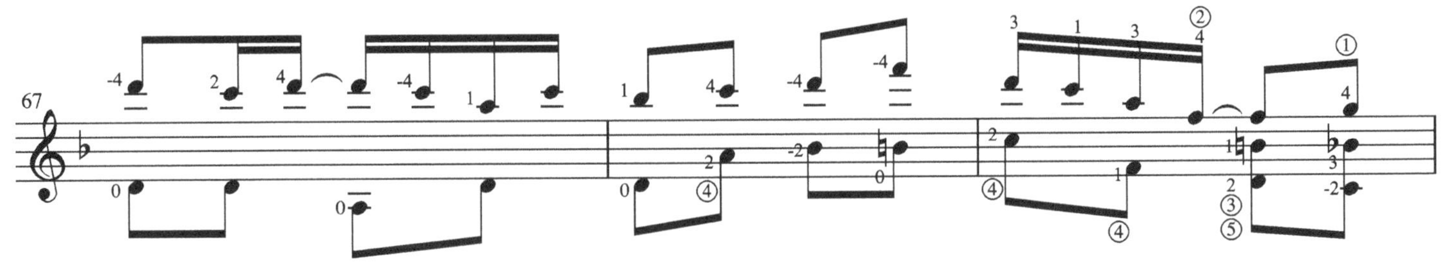

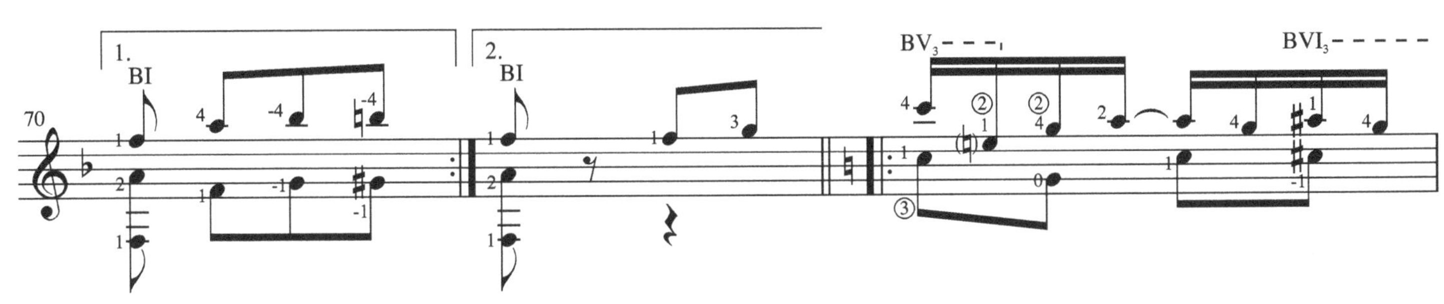

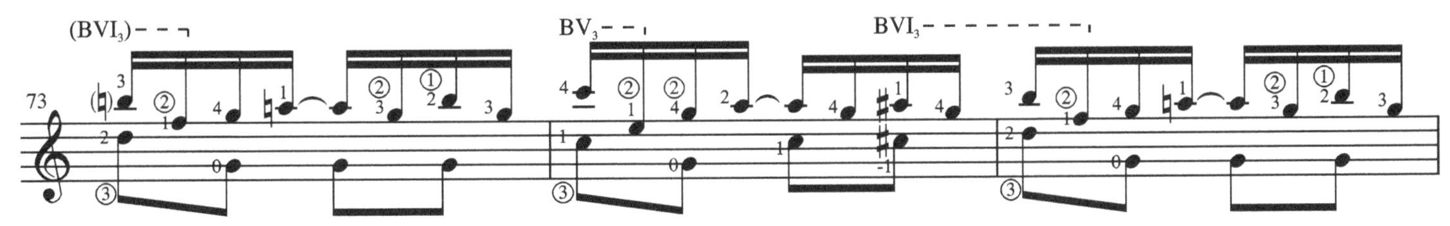

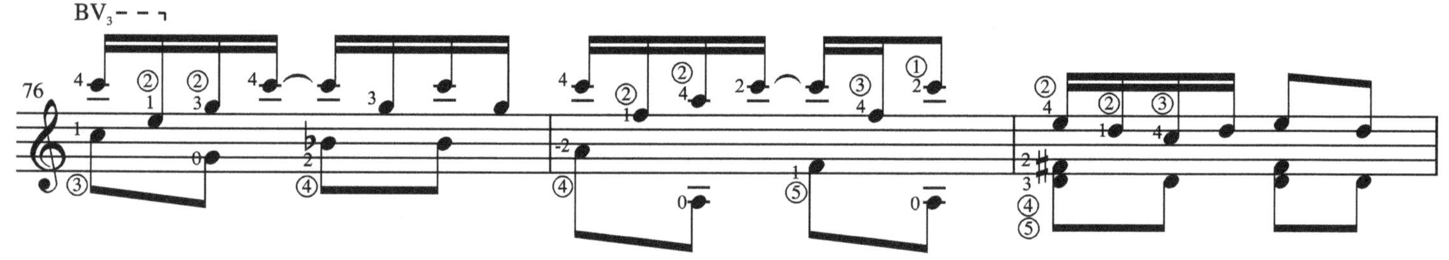

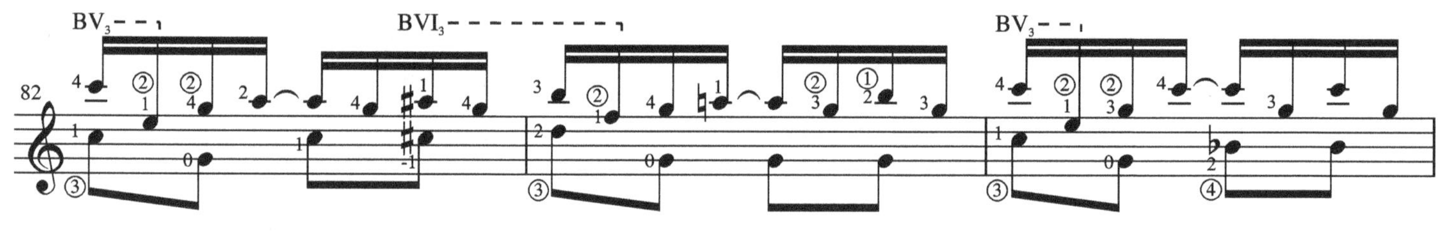

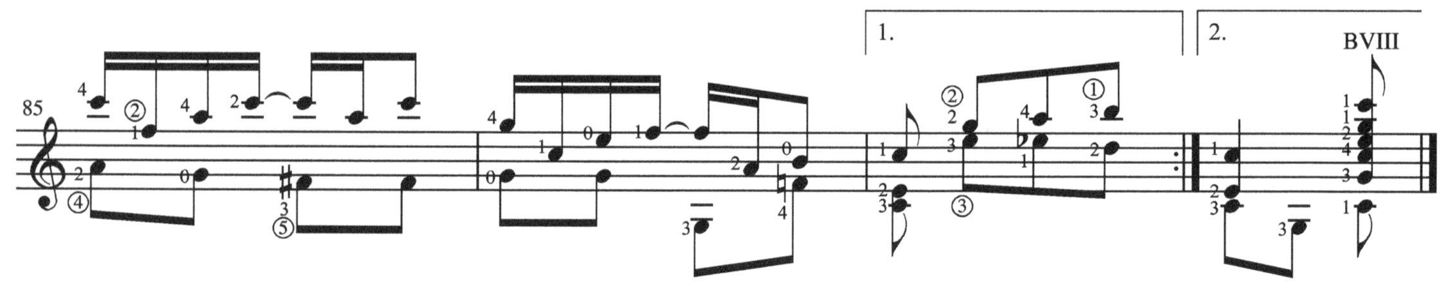